From Zero to Hero Caregiver

How to Effectively Prevent and Manage Caregiver Burnout

Annissa Fadaz

"I once had a lady in my practice (l will call her Sarah to protect her identity). Sarah was a widowed 50-year-old single mother of four. All four kids had various physical and mental ailments, including severe obesity, hypertension, kidney disease, high cholesterol, and poor self-esteem. Two of her children were diagnosed with severe anxiety and depression. One child had an extensive history of self-harm and violence at age 14. As if this wasn't enough, Sarah learned that her 11-year-old daughter was a victim of sexual abuse at school, and this had been going for at least 18 months. Sarah herself suffered from obesity and osteoarthritis with reduced mobility.

With everything that was happening, Sarah reached out to close friends, community services, healthcare professionals, and legal services. She even sought help from the media to get the attention and support she needed for her children and herself, unfortunately, without results.

Sarah did her best to cope and stay strong for her family, juggling the tasks of motherhood and caregiving. But watching their lives going downhill, she started breaking down. She began feeling more and more helpless and pessimistic. All she could see was a gloomy, dark future for herself and her loved ones."

Sadly, there are millions of caregivers like Sarah, who are going through hardships and setbacks while caring for others.

Without practical tools and relevant knowledge, Caregiving can be emotionally, physically, mentally, and spiritually draining to the point of Burnout.

The purpose of this book is to provide new and experienced Primary Caregivers with simple instructions, effective tools, and coping strategies to identify and avoid Caregiver Burnout. It is intended to be as interactive as possible so that you, as a Caregiver, feel actively involved and empowered.

This book is divided into four sections. In the first chapter, I review the definition of Burnout and share common causes that expose Carers to Burnout. In the second and third chapters, I provide questionnaires to help Caregivers assess their risks for Burnout. I've also included a screening tool to detect Burnout. The last section is about tips to prevent and manage a Burnout.

Please, make sure to download your FREE Caregiver's planner and daily-log to help you organize your daily tasks and keep track of your loved ones' needs.

About the author:

Annissa Fadaz is a trained Physician who has been practicing Family Medicine in Ontario, Canada, since 2011. With a medical degree from the University of Lome, Togo, she completed her Family Medicine Residency at the University of Ottawa, Canada. More than 40,000 encounters with patients and Caregivers have helped Annissa develop a deep understanding of the intricacies and challenges of providing chronic care. Annissa is passionate about finding innovative and empowering solutions to improve the care provided to patients and enhance a Caregiver's experience.

Table of Contents

1.

What is Caregiver Burnout?

A Burnout is a state of physical, emotional, mental, and even spiritual depletion arising from longstanding work-related stress. Burnout is not an official medical diagnosis. Rather, it is a "phenomenon" related to a strenuous workload and unrealistic expectations. The term is commonly used in the professional setting for trained healthcare professionals. It has been tacitly extended to describe the distress experienced by Primary Caregivers.

Some of the other terms used to describe Caregiver Burnout are primary caregiver fatigue and caregiver stress.

About 50% of Primary Caregivers (also called Informal Caregivers) experience emotional distress and Burnout somewhere in their journey. Studies show that this number is higher among those who provide more than 21 hours of care per week and those attending to a sick relative for 4 years or more. The condition of the person receiving the care also plays an important role in the risk of Caregiver Burnout.

Caregivers with Burnout often experience intense fatigue and exhaustion that can linger for weeks, months, and even years. There is a feeling of negativity towards caregiving tasks, sometimes leading to resentment. Over time, this can affect the caregiver's performance.

Oftentimes, other stressful aspects of Caregiver life contribute to distress, such as personal financial stress, marital problems, single parenthood or attending to a sick loved one while holding down a job.

Caregiver Burnout differs from mental conditions like Anxiety and Depression. A Caregiver experiencing a Burnout doesn't have excessive worries or pervasive fears about all aspects of life.

Caregivers can experience depression, characterized by deep sadness and persistently depressed mood with a negative impact on all areas of life (i.e., work, family life, and relationships with loved ones). There may be suicidal or homicidal thoughts in the case of depression, which is not seen in Burnout.

Another critical difference is that with Burnout, the changes reported (fatigue, reduced performance, negativism) only affect the domain of Caregiving. They typically don't spill over to other areas of life, especially at the initial phase of a Burnout. As the Burnout progresses, other domains such as relationships with the care recipient and other people may be affected. In such cases, it becomes necessary to screen for mental disorders like Anxiety and Depression.

If you have decided to dig into this book, chances are that you're concerned about Caregiver Burnout. If that case, it is essential to assess your burnout risk score and screen for Caregiver Burnout. In the following chapters, I'm going to share a self-assessment tool that will help you evaluate your risk factors. I'll also provide a self-screening tool for Caregiver Burnout. The last section of this book includes tips and advice on managing and preventing Caregiver Burnout.

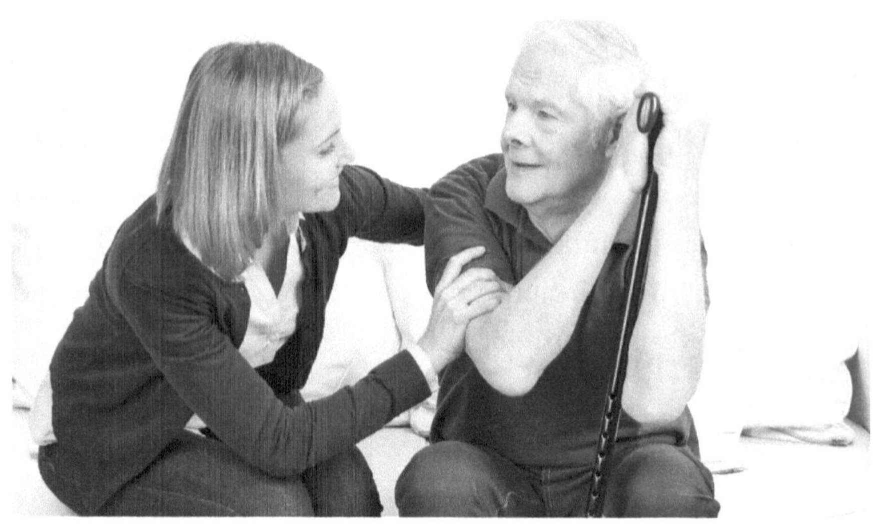

2.

Are You at Risk for Caregiver Burnout?

STRENUOUS STRESS: A MAJOR RISK FACTOR FOR BURNOUT

Strenuous **STRESS** is the number one risk factor for Burnout. Stress is defined as "a normal reaction to change that requires an adjustment or response."

When we're under stress, chemicals are released in our brains and bodies in response to external or internal stimuli. The effect of the reaction can be physical, emotional, mental, and even spiritual. Everybody experiences stress. It is a normal part of life. Stress can actually be beneficial – it can make us more focused, alert, motivated, and productive.

Stress becomes harmful when it occurs continuously without intervening periods of relief. People who feel constantly pressured,

10

those who are overwhelmed by their work, or those who experience internal turmoil are prone to the adverse effects of stress.

Informal caregiving (voluntarily caring for a friend or relative with disability or illness) puts the Caregiver under stress. A condition called "spouse burnout syndrome" has been described where the spouse of a chronically ill patient shows burnout symptoms comparable to those experienced by professional caregivers. Stress can lead to emotional exhaustion (feeling drained and unable to continue) and depersonalization (feeling detached and putting emotional distance between yourself and the person you're caring for).

CAREGIVER BURNOUT RISK SELF-ASSESSMENT QUESTIONNAIRE

This is a 20-point self-assessment quiz to assess your risk for Caregiver Burnout. Answer each question with a yes or no. Add 1 point for each yes and 0 for each no. Check "not applicable" if you feel the statement is not relevant to your situation. Count your points at the end to get your total score. Then go to the section "Assess Your Score."

Check if you are at risk of Caregiver Burnout by completing the following questionnaire:

Statement	Yes	No	Not applicable
1. High caregiver workload (You provide more than 21 hours of caregiving services every week; you care for your sick relative overnight)			
2. Lack of appreciation (You don't feel appreciated as a Caregiver for the help you provide to your sick relative)			
3. Lack of control (You don't make decisions regarding your Caregiver duties)			
4. Over-identification with the Caregiver role (You don't have boundaries when it comes to caregiving. The caregiver role takes over all aspects of your life)			
5. Unrealistic expectations (You feel only you can provide the care your loved one needs; you don't typically delegate Caregiving tasks)			
6. Parenthood (You are a parent with a child or children while supporting a loved one as a Caregiver)			
7. Employment (You work part-time or full-time while providing care to a sick relative)			
8. Social or scholar commitment (You volunteer or are enrolled in an educational institution while attending to a loved one)			
9. Financial pressure (You have financial problems and are unable to make ends meet)			

10. Personal sickness (You have mental and/or physical disorders)			
11. Isolation (You live alone, you have no friends or family, you lack community support)			
12. Caregiver gender (You are a woman)			
13. Distance (You live more than one hour away from the person you care for)			
14. Poor relations with your sick relative (You have relationship problems with the person you care for)			
15. Complex medical conditions (Your sick relative has more than 3 medical conditions; your relative has been sick for more than a year; your sick relative has complex medical needs requiring around-the-clock attention)			
16. Care recipient with poor social support (Your sick relative has limited social support and it's your responsibility to find additional help in the community)			
17. Care recipient with poor financial situation (Your sick relative has financial problems)			
18. Care recipient with legal concerns (Your sick relative has legal problems and needs your help to sort them out)			
19. Care recipient's unrealistic expectations (Your sick relative expects you to be present 24/7 to provide care without respite)			

20. Difference of cultural and value systems (You have a different value system and/or cultural background with your relative which often leads to clashes)			

Assess Your Score:

- Less than or equal to 2 points: You have a low risk for Caregiver Burnout. You may still want to check the next section about Caregiver Burnout detection and review the tools provided in the last chapter on prevention and management.

- From 3 to 7 points: You have a moderate risk for Caregiver Burnout – Please assess your Caregiver Burnout Score in the following section and check the Caregiver Burnout management and prevention tools in the last section.

- Above 8 points: Your risk of Caregiver Burnout is High – Please assess your Caregiver Burnout Score and review the Caregiver Burnout management and prevention tools in the last section. You may also benefit from a consultation with a healthcare provider to assess your health and mental state. Consider talking to a community service agent to discuss the need for support.

3.

Do You Have Caregiver Burnout?

This is a 15-point self-questionnaire divided into 3 sections.

Answer each question to the best of your abilities with a yes or no. I have provided an example with each item, in case you need clarification.

Scoring System: Give yourself 1 point for each yes and 0 for each no. Check "not applicable" if you feel the statement is not relevant to your situation. At the end of each section, count your points and move on to the next section.

Over the past 2 weeks, have you experienced:

SECTION 1

Statement	Yes	No	Not applicable
1. Fatigue, energy depletion, exhaustion, tired easily *For example, you feel extremely tired even though you just slept or performed minimal activities.* *You don't feel rested even after a nap.*			
2. Resentment/cynicism towards caregiving, and sometimes, towards your sick relative *You despise Caregiver duties such as buying groceries, cooking, cleaning, or driving your sick relative around.* *You feel disgusted by Caregiving tasks such as changing adult incontinence garments or helping your relative with bathing or feeding.* *You despise your sick relative.*			
3. Inability to assume regular responsibilities, lack of performance *You feel your level of commitment and/or efficiency is decreasing.* *You are not as fast as you used to be. It takes you longer to get things done.* *You have decreased productivity, reduced efficiency, and the inability to cope with daily activities related to Caregiving (i.e., administrative duties, obtaining communities resources, personal care).*			
Section 1 Total Score =			

SECTION 2			
Statement	Yes	No	Not applicable
4. Change in sleeping and eating patterns *You have experienced a shift in sleeping patterns with reduced sleep or a tendency to oversleep without feeling rested. You have difficulties falling asleep. You experience frequent awakenings at night and do not feel rested after a night of sleep. Your sleep is shallow and agitated.* *There is a change in appetite or eating habits. You notice you tend to eat less or more, binge eat, or have cravings for certain foods, i.e., junk foods and sweets.*			
5. Self-medicating with recreational drugs, alcohol misuse, resuming or increasing smoking *You use street drugs such as marijuana or cocaine to cope with your day.* *You find yourself smoking cigarettes and your consumption has increased recently.* *You use alcohol to escape from Caregiving duties. You find yourself drinking more recently.* *You are using more prescription drugs like painkillers or sleeping pills because you are in pain or have difficulty sleeping due to caregiving.*			
6. Lack of concentration, memory loss, declining intellectual performance *You have a hard time focusing on tasks. Your mind tends to wander. You need to read something multiple times to grasp the topic. You find yourself repeating some tasks or not feeling confident about the results. You are unable to make effective and quick decisions like before.*			

7. Irritability and frustration *You are often irritated and experience sudden mood swings. You are easily triggered by noise in your environment or by comments and behaviours from people in your entourage. You occasionally feel nervous and on-edge and experience bursts of anger.*			
8. Physical changes *You find you are getting sick more often or more easily. You are catching all the bugs that come around while others in your entourage seem to be doing ok. You experience recurrent headaches, upset stomach, or palpitations. You need to take more sick days from your job.*			
Section 2 Total Score =			

SECTION 3			
Statement	Yes	No	Not applicable
9. Progressive or sudden withdrawal from family and friends *You feel the urge to extract yourself from social and family interactions. You are frequently annoyed or exasperated. You feel challenged in social situations. You isolate yourself.*			
10. Lack of motivation, loss of interest in previously enjoyable activities *There is a progressive lack of interest in activities and hobbies you previously enjoyed. Participating in any event or hobby feels pointless and oppressive.*			
11. Persistence of deep sadness and depressed mood *You feel down and your mood is low most of the time. Nothing cheers you up.* *You feel hopeless and helpless and can't cope with life anymore.*			
12. Constant worries and pervasive fears *Your thoughts are constantly racing. You feel overwhelmed by your thoughts. You find it difficult to quiet your mind.* *You worry about everything… your work, your dog, your spouse, the kids, the neighbour, what's going in the world…* *Everything seems to affect you personally and you feel burdened by everything that's going on.* *You anticipate the worst in every situation (or many situations), even though there is no serious or imminent danger.*			

13. Feeling constantly nervous, anxious, or on-edge			
You feel restless, easily irritable, nervous. This may or may not be related to a stressful situation you are currently experiencing. You have difficulty calming yourself. *You have trouble letting go, relaxing, enjoying doing nothing. Your mind is constantly chasing thought after thought. You are unable to feel calm and at peace.* *You are fidgety and impatient. Staying quiet for a few minutes is a challenge. You feel the urge to constantly be on the move.*			
14. Suicidal thoughts *You have thoughts to harm yourself.* *You want to kill yourself and have a clear plan to proceed.*			
15. Homicidal intents *You want to hurt someone and have a clear plan to proceed.*			
Section 3 Total Score =			

SECTION 1:

- If you scored 0 for the entire questionnaire, you likely don't have Caregiver Burnout or mental illness.
- If you scored 1 or 2 for Section 1 - You likely have burnout.
- If you scored 3 points - You have a burnout.
- You should go to the last chapter of this book for some tips on preventing and managing Caregiver Burnout.

SECTION 2:

- This section explores the impact of Burnout on some aspects of your life.
- If you scored any points in section 2, you may have a more severe case of Burnout.
- I suggest you review the last chapter for some insights on how to manage Caregiver Burnout. I also recommend you seek medical and psychological care as you may be at risk for mental illness.

SECTION 3:

- This section screens for mental illnesses such as anxiety and depression.
- If you scored any point in section 3, you may have a mental disorder.

- Your condition could be severe. The tools in this book may not be sufficient or appropriate for you.
- I strongly recommend you seek medical attention.
- If you checked yes for point #14 and/or #15, please call your mental crisis line as you are at risk for self-harm or harm to others which requires immediate attention and care. If you live in North America, you can also call 911 or go to the nearest hospital.

4.

How to Prevent and Manage
Caregiver Burnout?

Caregiver Burnout is preventable.

Some practical tools and tips can help you, the Caregiver, prevent a Burnout or effectively manage it.

The good news is that most of the tips to prevent a Burnout are also helpful if you're already suffering from it.

Assessing, Planning, Delegating, and Self-Care are the four key elements of Burnout prevention and management.

Let's review together the steps you can take to prevent a Burnout or manage it.

1. Ask for Help

If you're a long-term Caregiver and feel overloaded, or even if you're just starting your Caregiver journey, it is essential to think about getting help. Don't isolate yourself. Isolation is one of the most common risk factors for major mental and physical illnesses. As much as possible, get in touch with someone you trust and open up about your situation. Reach out to local support groups or community services to help you through this difficult phase.

Tip: If you have limited community contact, you may want to reach out to:

- Local caregiver supports groups: Search on Google for groups in your area.
- Not-for-profit organizations: Some North American agencies are Carers Canada, National Alliance for Caregiving (NAC), and AARP (American Association for Retired People).
- Religious communities: You could reach out to local Christian, Muslim or other confessional organizations for support.
- Local community support services: You can ask a healthcare provider, municipality, or city hall for contact information.
- Healthcare provider: You can get in touch with your healthcare provider to assess your overall health. They may offer you additional information and support pertaining to your specific situation. Your healthcare professional may suggest you take a break from Caregiving.

Think about taking a break. The more you overstretch yourself, the more tired you will feel. Consider hiring a professional caregiver for respite care.

Tip: Here are a few steps to follow during the hiring process.

- **Make an inventory of your loved one's needs:** Your Care Plan should include an outline of your relative's medical conditions, treatments, prognosis, and goals of care. Involve the care recipient in the hiring process, if possible. Think about the personal qualities you would like the paid Caregiver to have.

- **Review employment requirements:** Each country or state has specific employment requirements. Find out your rights and duties as an employer. Relevant information is available on Google or from your municipality or city hall.

- **Write a job description:** Clearly outline the technical competencies, experience, and interpersonal skills (how the paid caregiver interacts with others), and values your ideal candidate should have. Ask for references. Be clear, concise, and specific in your job description.

- **Use an agency or do it yourself:** You can hire a professional caregiver through an agency or post the job online or on your social networks (word of mouth, social media, etc.). Each hiring method has advantages and disadvantages. Choose the one that suits you better. Agencies offer peace of mind. You don't have to go through candidate applications. You have a plan B if one caregiver doesn't work out. At the same time, agencies are more expensive and lack flexibility. When you do it yourself, you can communicate directly with the candidates and choose the best person. It will also be cheaper.

- **Review candidates and conduct interviews:** Interviews are part of the hiring process whichever way you go. If you use an agency, you will want to "interview" the people who run it. If you do it yourself, you'll interview candidates. It is impossible to judge a book by its cover, but a face-to-face interview will allow you to assess the caregiver's professionalism, punctuality, politeness, and tidiness. You'll get a sense of what it will be like to work with them. Assess their values, professionalism, technical abilities, and interpersonal skills. You should feel comfortable in the presence of a paid Caregiver. Review resumes and motivation letters in detail. Discuss any confusion and seek clarifications. You may perform a technical assessment of their competencies. For example, you could ask the potential Caregiver to perform specific tasks and assess their skills (check if this is allowed in your jurisdiction). Some employers ask for proof of training and experience (diplomas, evidence of past employment). Ask for a recent criminal record for the vulnerable sector (if this document is available in your area). Ask for proof of CPR and First Aid training. Check their ID and work permit. Most importantly, check references. In my opinion, it is better to cross-check references and discuss them in person instead of over the phone (when possible). Many candidates will also want to get to know you and see if you will be a good match.

APPLY FOR ASSISTED LIVING FOR YOUR LOVED ONE

The tips for hiring a paid caregiver are also applicable to choosing an assisted living facility. You will probably need to consult your loved one's doctor for better clarity about their health conditions and the type of assisted living that will be appropriate for their needs. The healthcare professional and social services can help you find the right place for your loved one.

3. CARE PLAN

A Care Plan is an essential tool for effective Caregiving. You should also think about a Care Team. Ideally, a Care Team consists of close friends, relatives, and neighbours who can help. I suggest you have as many team members involved as possible. They will be the ones carrying out responsibilities and tasks alongside you, the Primary Caregiver.

Have a structure in place. Divide your plan into sub-sections. Outline precise functions under each category. There should be a detailed description of tasks, a timeframe for their completion, as well as ways to check for accountability.

Think about plan Bs if the initial programs don't work out. For example, if one of your nieces was assigned to complete a specific task, and for some reason she isn't able to, who will take over? The plan should include the overall goals of care as well as the aspects of life that are key to your loved one's wellbeing. Here are some elements you can consider including in your Care Plan.

Heath Assessment

Gather this information as part of your loved one's health assessment. Place a checkmark against the information once you have collected it:

Type of information	Info collected	Info not applicable
1. Current and past medical conditions (provided by your relative's doctor)		
Allergies (provided by your loved one or their doctor or pharmacist)		
Current medications (updated list provided by your relative's pharmacist)		
Lifestyle (smoking, alcohol use, recreational drug use, diet, physical activity (if applicable), caffeine consumption)		
List of all healthcare professionals involved in your loved one's care with their contact information		
Insurance company contact and certificate numbers		
Do Not Resuscitate (DNR) status		
Power of Attorney contact information		
Care team members names and contact information		

Below is a framework for daily activities and needs assessment:

You can use the tools known as ADLs (Activities of Daily Living) or IADLs (Instrumental Activities of Daily Living) to make an inventory of your loved one's needs.

IADLs stands for Instrumental Activities of Daily Living. There is an established list of 7 components on adult caregiving. Check each required item. Use the extra space to list your own specific items.

My relative needs help with	Yes	No	Person(s) Responsible
Managing finances Paying bills, managing financial assets…			
Managing transportation Driving or organizing transport to attend medical, legal appointments…			
Shopping Doing groceries, buying clothes…			
Housecleaning, housekeeping Laundry, dishes, home maintenance…			
Cooking/meal preparation			
Managing medications and/or injections Obtaining and renewing medications, organizing, storing, dispensing medications, supervising and making sure medications are taken as directed, following up with healthcare professionals to get medications updated…			

Arranging outside services Searching for local resources, community outreach, hiring and managing paid caregivers/homeworkers, scheduling appointments, care coordination, managing communication, reaching out via telephone and mail to address legal matters…			

ADLs stands for Activities of Daily Living. Check each required item.

My relative needs help with	Yes	No	Person(s) Responsible
Walking/mobilizing The ability to get from point A to point B and may include climbing stairs.			
Feeding This can involve cutting meats and/or bringing utensils to the person's mouth.			
Dressing and grooming Selecting clothes, putting them on, and adequately managing the care recipient's personal appearance.			
Toileting Getting to and from the toilet, using it appropriately, maintaining hygiene, dealing with incontinence or diapers.			

Bathing or showering Washing the care recipient's face and/or body in a bathtub or shower.			
Transferring Moving the person from one position to another. This includes moving the person from bed to chair or wheelchair or standing position.			

Again, it is essential to add a detailed list of medical conditions and treatments as well as the contact information for healthcare professionals (family doctor, pharmacist, physical therapist…) to your Care Plan.

These lists should be available to everyone involved in the "Circle of Care" (aka your Care Team). A schedule of all appointments should be accessible to every Caregiver as well.

Think about your loved one's medications. How will the drugs be organized, stored, and dispensed? Will your loved one need somebody to supervise intake of medicines? If so, who? If there is any question related to medications, you should contact the pharmacist or the doctor who prescribed them.

Think about regular follow-ups with healthcare professionals, either in person or over the phone (when available). Within your Care Team, choose one person who is responsible for carrying out these tasks.

Sometimes you may be asked to make a judgement call on your loved one's mental state or ability to drive. If you have questions, reach out to a healthcare professional (for example, their doctor).

Home Assessment or Home Readiness

For care recipients who live at home, it is essential to assess the readiness of the house. This should be done inside-out, with a comprehensive checklist of anything that could be a potential safety risk or health hazard. For example, an elderly parent with reduced mobility may be safest in one-level housing (a bungalow or first-level apartment). You will need to check whether proper railings are in place, check staircase safety, assess electrical hazards, and make sure the floors are even. You may need to install alarm systems or better lighting in the house. It may be useful to have an occupational therapist, physiotherapist, or security expert involved in the assessment.

It's important to remember that Caregiving is ultimately about making life comfortable and safe for your loved one. Don't get carried away in planning for home readiness and forget to obtain input from the care receiver. Involve your loved one when you're preparing their living space. Ask for their suggestions on home modifications. You'll gain insight into their situation and may learn about unmet needs or unnecessary equipment.

Besides your loved one's personal space, you'll need to make every room in the home as accident-proof as possible. Every care receiver's situation is different. Someone with very limited mobility may never go into the kitchen, for example, and kitchen safety may be a moot point. Another care receiver may be quite independent and able to live alone, but may require home modifications to stay safe. Here's a room-by-room checklist to help you assess your loved one's home environment for potential safety concerns.

Entrance/Exit

- o Is the entrance/exit free of clutter and well lit?
- o Are there safety railings on the ramp and stairs?
- o Is there any uneven flooring or loose boards?
- o Does the door lock work?
- o Is there an emergency exit and fire escape?
- o Can visitors be screened before being allowed to enter the home?

Living area

- o Are there clear pathways between the various living spaces?
- o Is there any unnecessary clutter?
- o Is there a comfortable chair or sofa on which your loved one can sit and get up easily? (Height adjustments, additional cushions, etc. may be necessary).
- o Is everything within easy reach (TV remote, lamps, light switches)?
- o Are there any loose electrical/telephone cords or throw rugs?
- o Can anything be adapted to make life easier (for example, a telephone instrument with larger buttons)?

Kitchen

- o Are the cabinets at an accessible height?
- o Are sharp objects like knives and scissors stored safely?
- o Do the appliances work properly?
- o Are the electrical outlets within reach of the appliances?
- o Is there adequate countertop space for food preparation?
- o Are the faucets easy to manipulate?

o   Are the freezer and refrigerator accessible?

o   Are pots, pans, and utensils within easy reach?

o   Are there any fire hazards such as curtains or towels near the stove or cooking range?

Bedroom

o   Is the bed safe to get in and out of? (You may need to add a trapeze bar or consider purchasing an electric bed).

o   Can the phone be reached from the bed?

o   Are there light switches within reach from the bed?

o   Is there a well-lit, clutter-free path to the bathroom?

o   Can clothing in the dresser or cupboard be accessed easily?

Bathroom

o   Is the shower or bathtub safe to get in and out of? (You may need to install grab bars).

o   Will your loved one benefit from a shower chair or tub bench?

o   Is there a non-slip mat or non-skid strips on the floor?

o   Can your loved one safely and hygienically use the toilet? (You may need to add grab bars).

o   Is the water thermostat set low to prevent burns?

o   Are the light switches within easy reach?

o   Is the bathroom well-lit? Is there a nightlight?

o   Is the bathroom rug secured in place with adhesive tape?

o   Is there a telephone in the bathroom for emergencies?

Staircase

o   Does the stairway have a safety rail on both sides?

o   Is the flooring of the staircase non-slip or the carpet secure?

o   Is there any unnecessary clutter that can be removed from the stairs?

General

o   Are the smoke detectors in working order?

o   Are there any fire hazards like electrical blankets or space heaters? (If so, you may need to remove them or place them away from flammable rugs, curtains, furniture, and papers).

o   Are electrical cords in good condition? (You should replace anything that appears damaged or frayed).

o   Is the home well lit with nightlights in the hallways?

o   Are the rugs secured in place? (You may need to remove rugs if your loved one uses a walker or wheelchair).

o   Has the home been checked for insects and other household pests?

o   Are all the utilities in working order? Is the plumbing in good condition?

o   Is the phone accessible to your loved one in all areas of the home?

o   Are emergency numbers posted clearly in a central area?

o   Are medicines stored safely with proper labels?

Financial Assessment

As a Caregiver, you may have to carry out the role of a Financial Power of Attorney for your loved one. I suggest you review their overall economic situation and go through their assets and liabilities in preparation for the future. You may want to involve a financial advisor to guide you with this.

Social/Community Involvement Assessment

If you decide to take part in community activities with your loved one, it may be useful to reach out to social or community experts to help you with the planning and execution of activities and events. Which events will you be attending? In which setting? Will you have to arrange transportation for your loved one? These are some of the questions you should consider.

Legal Documents

These include wills, trusts, and POA (Power of Attorney) documents for personal care, medical or health care, financial decision making, HIPAA authorization documents or medical release documentation, and advance healthcare directives. It is advisable to seek legal advice and maybe think about having an attorney in your Care Team.

Training

Research shows that up to 57% of Caregivers perform nursing tasks as part of their duties. Many feel unprepared for their new role. Getting caregiving-related training is an efficient way to prevent Burnout. So, think about obtaining relevant training to be more effective as a Caregiver.

Remember, writing a Care Plan is a dynamic process. More likely than not, you and your Care Team will have to reassess, rewrite, remove/add some sections as you go along, and that's okay. Be open and flexible with any changes that come your way.

Please, make sure to download your FREE Caregiver's planner and daily-log to help you organize your daily tasks and keep track of your loved ones' needs.

4. DELEGATE TO YOUR CARE TEAM

You may be familiar with the phrase, "No man is an island."

It is certainly true when it comes to Caregiving. Caregivers who experience isolation and lack of support are more prone to mental and physical ailments.

Tip: Your Care Team should include several people. Here's a quick list you can go through:
- o Nurse(s)
- o Personal support worker(s), Paid caregiver(s)
- o Community agent(s), Social worker(s)
- o Geriatric (case) assessor/ manager
- o Doctors (specialists, family doctor)
- o Physiotherapist, massage therapist, chiropractor
- o Nutritionist, dietician
- o Occupational therapist
- o Speech therapist
- o Housekeeper
- o Handyman
- o Administrator
- o Financial advisor
- o Lawyer

Self-care is paramount to Burnout management and prevention. Self-care is not being selfish. It is an intelligent and wise approach to Caregiving. The more balanced and harmonious your life is, the better your Caregiving experience.

In the following sections, I am sharing a framework of 8 areas of life. You can use it to assess your overall health and wellness and implement changes accordingly.

I added few self-reflective questions to help you with your assessment, as well as some tips to expand the area of concern.

1. Spirituality & personal growth

The concept of spirituality has evolved. Now, there are many ways to refer to spirituality. It can be defined as how one relates to the Divine or Sacred or the beliefs by which you choose to live. Nowadays, spirituality has expanded well beyond religious practices.

Self-reflective questions: What are my sources of hope, strength, comfort and peace? What do I hold on to during challenging times?

2. Mind & emotions

The mind is a complex concept. Simply put, it is the way "one thinks." A term that is used to describe it is "cognition." Cognitive abilities are mental processes that you use to gather, process, analyze and store information. They are also your capacity to think critically according to your experiences and beliefs. Emotions can be simply defined as the way "we feel." We feel happy, sad, angry, etc. Our feelings are connected to the way we think, to what we believe. When I believe everything is well, I feel joyful and peaceful. Our minds and emotions (and our bodies) are the filters through which we interact with ourselves, others, and our environment.

Self-reflective questions: What makes me feel happy? How am I nourishing my mind?

3. Body & environment

The body is the interface we use in the physical realm to interact with material things. We see, smell, listen, taste, touch using our physical senses to connect with our environment. Our bodies are the vehicles we use to move from one place to another or to do things according to our goals.

Self-reflective questions: What is my diet like? How often do I exercise? How is my sleep?

4. Love life & intimate relationships

(Skip this part if you are not in an intimate relationship).

Love is a basic human need. It is an intense feeling of deep affection, a great pleasure in someone or something. We all crave love for ourselves and one another. Studies show that children who lack love and intimate bonding in early childhood are at higher risk of mental health problems and have a lower chance of success later in life. Close relationships with select people, romantic feelings, and mutual affection have a profound impact on our physical, mental, emotional, and spiritual wellness. Research has shown that a broken heart can have disastrous effects. It can shake a person to the point of death.

Self-reflective questions: Is my relationship with my partner meaningful and nurturing? Is there any room for improvement?

5. Family & friends

This includes people we are related to by blood or lineage and also the group of persons we share a deep affection or sense of belonging. The meaningful connections we share with a few unique individuals help us flourish and move ahead in life.

Self-reflective questions: Are my relationships with relatives and friends meaningful and nurturing? Is there any room for improvement?

6. Career, calling, & life missions

Humans are purpose-driven beings. The Bible says: "Without vision, the people perish." As humans, we need a vision for our lives. Through our dreams and missions, we contribute to one another's experiences, becoming the answer to someone else's need or prayer.

Self-reflective questions: What are my dreams? Do I despise what I do? Do I have a sense of calling in life?

7. Finances & money

Money is the tool we use to acquire material things we need or want. The extent to which we will go to get money and how we use it is linked to our thinking and belief systems.

Self-reflective questions: What are my sources of income? What are my assets? What are my expenses? What are my liabilities? What are my debts?

8. Social & recreational life

We replenish and rejuvenate ourselves with enjoyable activities and fun. They help us lead more harmonious and balanced lives.

Self-reflective questions: What do I do for fun? What are my hobbies? Have I planned any social or recreational activity recently?

Tips for Self-Care

Here is a checklist of things you can do to expand each area of your life.

Enable spiritual growth
- o   Join a religious community
- o   Perform regular breathing exercises
- o   Meditate
- o   Sing
- o   Practice hobbies
- o   Spend time in nature
- o   Take care of animals
- o   Sit in silence
- o   Practise Tai Chi or Yoga

The list is endless…

Start a journey of self-discovery
- o   Identify your talents, passions, and dreams
- o   Cultivate a new passion
- o   Find a purpose in life
- o   Start writing a daily journal
- o   Actively seek new experiences

Take care of your senses

Our senses are filters to grasp the environment and enhance our cognitive abilities. Taking care of our physical senses is a way to care for our mind, emotions, and overall being.

- o Avoid watching or listening to programs that make you feel angry, lazy, or downcast.
- o Surround yourself with pleasant smells, a particular flower, for example.
- o Surround yourself with beauty.
- o Eat healthy, tasty foods that nourish your body, mind, emotions, and spirit.
- o Take care of your skin, the largest organ in your body. It protects you from harm, preserves your external defensive barrier, and promotes inner balance.

Learn new skills

Studies show that learning a new skill helps create new connections in the brain and promotes cognitive growth.

- o Learn to play an instrument
- o Learn a new craft
- o Play a new sport
- o Enrol in a new course
- o Start a DIY project

The list is endless…

Take care of your heath

- o Get enough sleep
- o Avoid stress
- o Eat healthy food
- o Exercise regularly
- o Avoid self-destructive behaviours, for example, stop smoking, stop indulging in things or people that do not help you grow.

Build meaningful connections

Make a concerted effort to build meaningful relationships. Don't remain in stagnant relationships that make you miserable. I know it's easier said than done, especially when it comes to family members, parents, and children. Do your best with what you have. Heal what can be healed, but remember that it takes two to tango. There is nothing you can do if you are the only one eager to salvage a relationship.

Conclusion

Caregiving is a rewarding yet challenging and transformative life experience. Self-awareness and knowledge of the risks that expose Caregivers to breakdowns are the keys to preventing and managing Burnout. Planning, delegation, and self-care are also vital to prevent Caregiver Burnout.

I hope this book has given you insights and practical tips to thrive as a Caregiver.

My best wishes to every single one of you on your journey.

Annissa Fadaz

Glossary

Definitions of terms used in the book:

1. Caregiver: Someone who helps a person with specific limitations and addresses their physical, emotional, mental, and social needs with the intention to improve overall health outcomes, provide comfort, alleviate pain, and/or provide a better quality of life. Caregivers include professionally trained healthcare providers as well as people who voluntarily take care of relatives for the sake of concern, compassion, dignity, and love.

2. Care recipient: A person with a mental or physical ailment or limitations who receives care or support.

3. Informal caregiving: Voluntary care for a loved one with disability or illness without receiving payment.

4. Primary caregiver: A member of the entourage providing care.

5. Family caregiver: A family member providing care to a sick relative.

6. Paid caregiver: A person who receives wages for providing care.

7. Professional caregiver: A person who is trained to provide care.

Resources

- https://www.aarp.org/content/dam/aarp/ppi/2015/caregiving-in-the-united-states-2015-reportrevised.pdf

- https://www.ncbi.nlm.nih.gov/pmc/articles/PMC5330336/

- https://www.ncbi.nlm.nih.gov/pmc/articles/PMC3537144/

- https://en.wikipedia.org/wiki/Spirituality#Contemporary_spirituality